Happiness Starts
Within
Me
Daily Journal

Jazmin Headley

Published by The Elite Lizzard Publishing Company

I believe
in myself
and
I trust
in my
abilities
to
succeed in
all I do.

Write something you are grateful for every day! Change starts today.

_____

_____

_____

_____

_____

_____

_____

_____

_____

_____

_____

_____

_____

_____

_____

_____

_____

_____

Draw something that makes you feel loved!

Behind every successful woman is herself!

The sky is the limit
when you put your mind to it.

Draw something that makes you smile!

Scars are beautiful.
They remind me of my
strength.

Draw 3 things that you are
grateful for today

What do you love about yourself?

She worked hard and her dreams came true!

Find something to do today that makes you feel good. Draw what you did!

It's the
little
things in
life that
matters
the
most

What is your favorite music or book that helps you relax?
Draw a self portrait

You get
in life what
you
have
the courage
to go after

We hope you feel so much joy and self love from writing in your daily journal.

Always remember this; You matter, you are enough and you are worthy of all the good things life has to offer!

www.ingramcontent.com/pod-product-compliance
Lightning Source LLC
Chambersburg PA
CBHW071014120626
46546CB00003B/1089